A family from
JAPAN

Simon Scoones

RSVP
RAINTREE
STECK-VAUGHN
PUBLISHERS
The Steck-Vaughn Company

Austin, Texas

FAMILIES AROUND THE WORLD

A family from **BOSNIA**

A family from **BRAZIL**

A family from **CHINA**

A family from **ETHIOPIA**

A family from **GERMANY**

A family from **GUATEMALA**

A family from **IRAQ**

A family from **JAPAN**

A family from **SOUTH AFRICA**

A family from **VIETNAM**

The family featured in this book is an average Japanese family. The Ukitas were chosen because they were typical of the majority of Japanese families in terms of income, housing, number of children, and lifestyle.

Cover: The Ukita family outside its home with all its possessions
Title page: Sayo hangs out the family's washing.
Contents page: Children run down the street in the local shopping area.

Picture Acknowledgments: All the photographs in this book were taken by Peter Menzel. The photographs were supplied by Material World/Impact Photos and were first published by Sierra Club Books in 1994 © Copyright Peter Menzel/Material World. The map artwork on page 4 is produced by Peter Bull.

Published by Raintree Steck-Vaughn Publishers, an imprint of Steck-Vaughn Company

Printed in Italy. Bound in the United States.
1 2 3 4 5 6 7 8 9 0 02 01 00 99 98

Library of Congress Cataloging-in-Publication Data
Scoones, Simon.
A family from Japan / Simon Scoones.
p. cm.—(Families around the world)
Includes bibliographical references and index.
Summary: Describes the activities of a Japanese family living in Tokyo, providing brief information about daily life and customs.
ISBN 0-8172-4909-5
1. Japan—Social life and customs—1945—Juvenile literature.
2. Family life—Japan—Juvenile literature.
3. Family—Japan—Juvenile literature.
[1.Family life—Japan. 2. Japan—Social life and customs.]
I. Title. II. Series: Families around the world.
DS822.5.S36   1998
306.85'0952—dc21   97-18295

Contents

Introduction

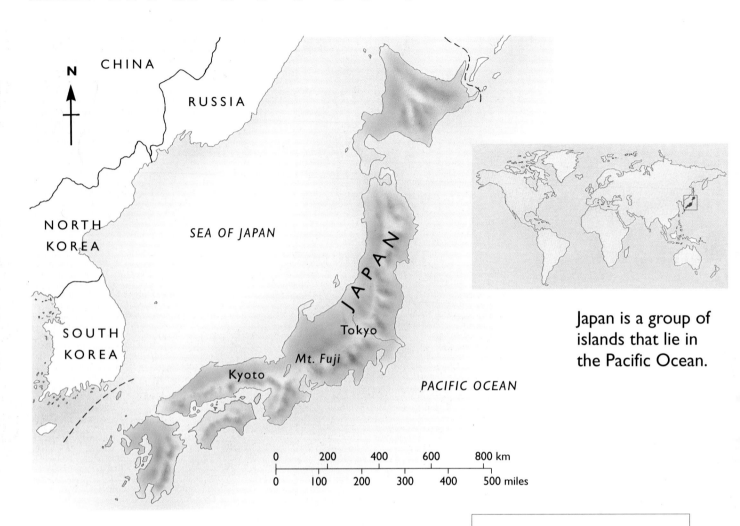

CHINA

RUSSIA

NORTH KOREA

SEA OF JAPAN

SOUTH KOREA

JAPAN

Tokyo

Mt. Fuji

Kyoto

PACIFIC OCEAN

N

0	200	400	600	800 km
0	100	200	300	400	500 miles

Japan is a group of islands that lie in the Pacific Ocean.

JAPAN

Capital city:	Tokyo
Size:	145,956 sq. mi. (377,997 sq. km)
Number of people:	125,900,000
Language:	Japanese
People:	Mostly Japanese, some Korean and Chinese
Religion:	Shinto, Buddhist, Confucianist, Christian
Currency:	Yen

THE UKITA FAMILY

Size of household:	4 people
Size of home:	1,420 sq. ft. (132 sq. m)
Workweek:	Kazuo: 40 hours
	Sayo: 60 hours (at home)
Most valued possessions:	Kazuo: Grandmother's ring
	Sayo: Grandfather's pottery
	Mio: Her unicycle
	Maya: Her dog, Izamaru
Family income:	$26,824

The Ukita family is a typical Japanese family. The Ukitas have put everything that they own outside their house so that this photograph could be taken.

Meet the Family

1 Kazuo, father, 45
2 Sayo, mother, 43

3 Mio, daughter, 9
4 Maya, daughter, 6

EARTHQUAKE!

Japanese people have learned to live with the danger of earthquakes. Long ago, people believed that earthquakes happened when a giant catfish shook its tail in the ocean.

The Ukita family lives in a small, two-story house on the edge of Tokyo, Japan's largest city. They only have to walk five minutes to reach Mio and Maya's grandparents' house. There is not much space in Tokyo, so houses are built close together. The Ukitas don't have a yard of their own, but there is a park close by.

"We have a normal-sized family for Japan today, but in the old days, families were much bigger. My mother had seven children including me."—*Sayo*

The Ukita House

The Ukitas' house has two floors. The bedrooms and bathroom are upstairs, and the kitchen and living room are downstairs.

CROWDED CITIES

Mountains cover most of Japan, so most Japanese people live on the flatter land along the coast. To make new pieces of land, engineers drain off water from the sea. In the cities, some roads are built on top of buildings because there is not enough room on the ground.

A Home of Their Own

Houses are expensive in Japan, so the Ukitas are lucky to own their home. The house has five small rooms, but it is modern and has everything that the family needs. The Ukita family owns another house in the countryside. Every few months, the Ukitas drive to their other house to enjoy the fresh air and open spaces.

The Latest Technology

The television in the living room has the latest technology. The remote control has a special button so that the family can listen to a program in either Japanese or English. Mio and Maya like to watch cartoons on television. Kazuo prefers to watch the sports programs.

Before bedtime, Mio likes to relax in front of the television with a cold drink.

Keeping Warm

Like most families in Japan, the Ukitas do not have heating in their house. When it is cold in the winter they have an extra pile of blankets to cover themselves and keep warm.

Bedrooms

Mio and her sister share a room in which there are bunk beds. Kazuo and Sayo sleep on a futon in their bedroom. A futon is a traditional type of bed that is made out of planks of wood and is covered with a mattress.

Mio's bedroom is the best place for peace and quiet. This is where she does her homework.

"We always take off our shoes before we go indoors. It shows respect for a person's home, and it also keeps the place clean!"—*Mio*

Food and Cooking

The Ukitas have a lot of machines to make life easier. Sayo finds the microwave very useful.

Choosing the Ingredients

Sayo is an excellent cook, and she makes sure the family is well fed. Luckily, Sayo has plenty of stores nearby, so she can spend time looking for the ingredients that she needs. The supermarket has plenty of choices, with food from all over the world. But Sayo usually buys fresh vegetables from the local store.

Breakfast

In the morning, Sayo prepares toast and coffee for the whole family. Sayo always makes sure the children eat breakfast before they go to school.

◀ Sayo stops at the supermarket for some last-minute dinner ingredients.

Sayo is proud of her kitchen. She always keeps it spotlessly clean.

Lunchtime

Mio and Maya have lunch at school with their classmates. Some Japanese food is quite unusual. Mio's favorite snack is a grasshopper cooked in soy sauce and sugar. It is delicious!

Manners

The girls know that it is important to have good table manners. Sticking your chopsticks upright in your rice is very rude in Japan.

Mio and her schoolfriends have lunch in one of the classrooms.

Family Supper

The evening meal is a good time for the family to sit down together and share the day's news. Before eating, the family says, *"itadakimasu"* to thank the people who produced the food. Sayo believes that it is important to arrange the food beautifully on each plate. She likes to make *sushimi*, which is raw fish on top of a bed of rice. Kazuo likes to eat his *sushimi* with *wasabi*. This is a spicy sauce made of herbs, horseradish, and soy sauce.

Sometimes the Ukitas like to watch television while they're eating.

Working Hard

MODERN TECHNOLOGY

Japanese companies are world-famous for making the latest designs in cars and electronics. Japanese televisions, stereos, cameras, cars, and kitchen equipment are sold all over the world.

Kazuo has lots of suits. He likes to look nice at work.

Kazuo works for a company that sells foreign books. He is always very busy checking that the right books have arrived. Kazuo likes to make sure that all his customers are happy.

Kazuo's brother is a special kind of doctor called an acupuncturist. He treats illnesses by pricking his patients' skin with needles. Acupuncture is an ancient kind of Chinese medicine.

Kazuo catches up on the news on his way to work.

> "The trains always run exactly on time. I usually reach the platform about a minute before my train arrives!"—*Kazuo*

Getting to Work

Kazuo's job is in the middle of Tokyo, so he has to travel to work by train. The journey takes an hour and a half, and he has to change trains twice.

"We don't have space to dry clothes indoors, so I use a special pole to hang my washing out the window. The wind does the rest of the work."—*Sayo*

Working at Home

Sayo is very busy at home. She gets up half an hour before everyone else to make the family's breakfast. Sayo takes a lot of care to make sure that the house is clean and tidy. At the end of the year, Mio and Maya help their mother to clean every corner of the house. This gives their home a fresh start for the new year to come.

Going Shopping

Sayo goes to the local stores twice a week to buy food for the family. Sometimes she bumps into her friends while she's shopping and stops to talk. Sayo finds it difficult to carry lots of bags of shopping, especially during hot weather.

Sayo mops the floor while the rest of the Ukitas are out. That way, no one will slip on the wet floor.

School Life

Mio gets lots of homework. She likes to have all her books near her desk.

STUDYING HARD

A school day in Japan starts at 8:30 A.M. and ends at 4:30 P.M. Children have to go to school on Saturdays. Many children take extra lessons in the evenings and on Saturday afternoons to help them pass very difficult exams.

Every morning, Sayo walks with Maya and Mio to their school to make sure that they get there safely. Each school day is seven hours long, although there are breaks during the day.

Maya and Mio both love sports. They really enjoy gym classes when they can play games such as volleyball and play on the ropes in the gym. During their break, Mio likes to skip rope while her friends sing and clap.

20

"Before school, I like to meet my friend, Akiko. Today, we're playing with her new camera."
—Maya

Passing Tests

Mio has to work very hard so that she can pass the examinations to get into a good junior high school next year. To improve her chances, Mio spends some time every evening doing her homework. On Saturday mornings, she attends *"juku,"* where she has extra lessons in the subjects that she finds more difficult.

Mio's teacher puts the best work of the class on the classroom walls.

Mio also enjoys her lessons in Japanese dance. She is practicing hard for a school show at the end of the year.

"I'm glad I don't have exams yet. My sister always has to work really hard."—*Maya.*

Starting School

Maya does not have to worry about examinations yet. She has only just started to go to school. Maya enjoys learning how to count and how to write the difficult Japanese alphabet.

Leisure and Play

Maya often practices playing the family piano.

HOLIDAYS

Many Japanese families spend their spare time in the mountains. There are beautiful waterfalls and the famous volcano, Mount Fuji. In the winter, there is enough snow for people to be able to ski. Japan also has its own Disneyland.

Getting Away

During the long summer vacation, the Ukitas sometimes go abroad. The family has already visited Europe and Hawaii. Someday, Sayo hopes to go to the United States to visit an old schoolfriend.

"I walk our dog in the park near our house. His name is Izamaru, and he is nearly as big as me!"—*Maya*

On Weekends

The Ukita family is often busy on weekends. Mio swims in the local swimming pool on Sunday mornings. She practices for two hours with 100 other children. Maya is learning how to play the piano and has lessons on Saturdays.

Mio wears goggles when she is swimming. They keep the water from stinging her eyes.

26

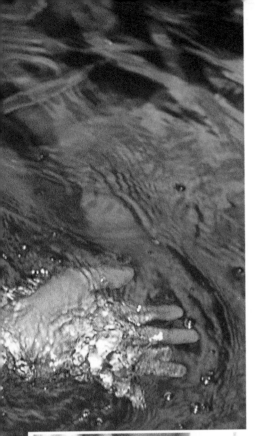

Meeting Friends

Kazuo likes to rest on Sundays, but sometimes he goes to a *karaoke* club with his friends. He enjoys singing along to his favorite songs, even though he sings completely out of tune!

▼ Kazuo enjoys a night out at a *karaoke* club.

 # The Future

Mio and her mother have fun when they go shopping.

A Change for Women

Mio and Maya both want to do well at school so that they will be able to have good jobs when they grow up. More women in Japan are choosing to have fewer children and to have jobs as well. The girls already have plans for their careers. Mio wants to be a doctor when she grows up, and Maya wants to be a famous musician.

School is finished for the day, so these children enjoy running down their local street.

Pronunciation Guide

Akiko	Ah-kee-koh
fugu	foo-goo
Fuji	Foo-jee
futon	foo-tahn
itadakimasu	ee-tah-dah-key-mah-sue
ízawaru	ee-zah-mah-rue
juku	joo-koo
karaoke	kah-rah-oh-key
Kazuo	Kah-zoo-oh
Kyoto	Ki-oh-toh
Maya	Mah-yah
Mio	Mee-oh

Sayo	Sah-yoh
sushimi	soo-shee-me
Tokyo	Toe-kee-oh
Ukita	You-key-tah
wasabi	wah-sah-bee

Glossary

Buddhism A religion followed by millions of people, mainly in Asia.

Chopsticks Made from wood, plastic, or metal, chopsticks are used for eating food instead of knives and forks.

Earthquakes A violent shaking of the earth's surface. Earthquakes can cause a lot of damage to people and buildings.

Electronics Modern machines that need electricity.

Emperor A ruler of a large area of land called an empire.

Engineers People who build roads, bridges, and buildings.

Juku Extra school lessons that happen at the weekends.

Karaoke A popular pastime in Japan, where people sing along to their favorite tunes.

Noodles Strips or rings of pasta, usually made with egg.

Province An area of a country.

Pufferfish A fish that can puff itself up to look like a spiky ball.

Volcano A mountain, usually cone-shaped, with a crater. Molten rock and hot ashes can be thrown out of the crater.

Volleyball A team game where the players push a ball over a net with their hands.

Books to Read

Bornoff, Nick. *Japan: City and Village Life* (Country Insights). Austin, TX: Raintree Steck-Vaughn, 1997.

Doran, Claire. *The Japanese* (Look Into the Past). Austin, TX: Thomson Learning, 1995.

Lerner Publications, Department of Geography Staff. *Japan in Pictures* (Visual Geography). Minneapolis, MN: Lerner Publications, 1994.

Tames, Richard and Sheila Tames. *Japan* (Country Topics for Craft Projects). Danbury, CT: Franklin Watts, 1995.

Index